table of

safety equipment

Working with resin can be a fun pastime However, before you go running off to create your first masterpiece, there are few things you need to consider. One of which is practicing resin safety.

MSDS

There are many different brands and types of resin on the market, so before you start, it is a good idea to know what you are dealing with. I recommend asking for the Manufacturer's Material Safety Data Sheets (MSDS). This will give you all the safety precautions you need for that particular resin.

RESPIRATOR

Even when the MSDS states that it is safe to work with resin without a respirator, I highly recommend that you do still wear one. Remember the Manufacturer's Safety Data Sheets only give information relating to the resin only. They don't take into consideration that as an artist you are likely to add other elements, like pigments, paint and other additives. Not to mention heating the resin with blow torches and heat guns. So always err on the side of caution.

VENTILATION

In addition to wearing the correct breathing equipment, it is also essential that the area in which you are working has good ventilation.

SAFETY GLASSES/GOGGLES

When working with resin it is also advisable to wear safety glasses or goggles. Your eyes can absorb fumes from heated resin plus they will protect you from airborne pigment particles and sanded resin.

DISPOSABLE GLOVES

Certain resins can react with disposable gloves, so we recommend the use of Nitrile Gloves. If you get resin on your hands or any other part of your body, use baby wipes to remove what you can.

Don't use any solvents or alcohol to remove the resin, this will help the resin absorb more quickly into your skin.

PROTECTIVE CLOTHING

Resin can easily penetrate through your clothing, so it is recommended that you wear old clothing and an apron. Also, only wear enclosed shoes, to avoid resin drips on your feet.

PROTECT YOUR AREA

It is always advisable to use plastic sheeting to protect your work area. Should you spill any resin, it is then easy to clean up. You can wait for the resin to cure and then peel it from the plastic. However, if the resin has dripped on to the floor, it is best to clean it straight away, to avoid walking it into other areas.

choosing a substrate

There are a variety of substrates that you can use to pour resin and of course, there are pros and cons to using each. Preparation is the key to gaining a good result

ARTIST CRADLE BOARDS

Artist's Cradle Boards and panels are usually made from birch and bought from an Art Shop. Birch is used as it provides an excellent surface for artists to paint on, plus the back is braced to prevent any warping, making them an excellent choice for resin.

You can pour resin directly on to these boards, however, I recommend always priming your boards before use. This not only protects the wood, but gives you a good base to start your resin pouring.

MDF BOARDS

MDF (Medium Density Fiberboard) is a cheaper alternative to Artist Cradle Boards. They come in a variety of thicknesses and can be purchased from your local hardware store. These are generally not braced on the back, however, your resin supplier may already have cradled boards or put you on to a supplier.

choosing a substrate

MDF continued

It is essential that you prime an MDF board, as it can easily absorb water and so over time can warp. I usually do two coats of primer on the front and back of the boards. I use a waterproof primer, just for added protection.

CANVAS

I am not a big fan of using canvas as a base for my resin art, however, I know that there are many people who prefer to use them as they are a cheaper alternative.

If using canvas, good preparation is essential to avoid sagging in the middle and resin pulling away from the edges.

First, your canvas needs to be as tight as possible. Lightly spray water on the back and use your hand to spread the water about and help it absorb into the material.

Leave it to dry, then add support to the back to prevent sagging. Many people use cardboard or pour a layer of resin on the back, in order to give a nice flat surface.

ACRYLIC/PLEXIGLAS

As acrylic and Plexiglas is a form of plastic and resin doesn't stick to plastic, it is not high on my list of recommendations. However, if like me you have a sheet lying around, then make sure you sand the surface to create a good 'tooth' for the resin to stick to.

Note, I have found after a while, the acrylic sheet I used had begun to bow in the centre. So I decided to keep this one for myself and don't plan to sell it.

GLASS

I have seen many people use glass as a substrate for resin and while it looks great, it can be a problem over time.

Glass bends and contracts at different rates to resin especially when exposed to different temperatures, meaning it can easily shatter and all your hard work could be lost.

I wouldn't recommend using glass!

TILES

Tiles are great for making coasters or trivets. Resin can be applied to both glazed and unglazed tiles. They can be bought from your local hardware store for a reasonable price.

There is no preparation required on tiles and so make a good option for those starting out with resin.

WOOD

Wood is great for working on, however, there are many factors to consider before applying the resin to wood.

If first needs to be dry, especially if you are using raw wood. Water and resin don't mix, so you need to make sure that your wood has been kiln dried before use.

I would recommend sealing the wood first, to prevent any 'out-gassing' when the resin is applied. If it is not sealed, it will not only absorb large amounts of your resin, it will cause bubbles to appear on the surface.

MELAMINE

Melamine is another surface that can take resin, like countertops or kitchen cupboard doors. As melamine is a form of plastic, the key to a good bond is in the preparation.

You will need to sand the surface to make sure ALL of the glossy coatings have been removed. Only then can you move on to the priming your surface before applying the resin.

TABLES

Resin tables look great, however, like when using raw wood, good preparation is essential for a flawless finish.

First, you need to sand back any coating that is on the surface of the wood and then apply a good primer. I find pouring a thin layer of resin and letting it cure, helps prevent bubbles escaping from the wood. It creates a great seal before applying your next layers.

preparing your board

As mentioned in the previous chapter, prepping your substrate is essential for a good finish and will avoid disappointment. In this chapter, I go into more detail on preparing a board to achieve different finishes, as this is mainly what people use for creating their resin art.

PRIMING

Priming gives your board not only a good background to work with, but it also prevents any moisture from penetrating in and warping your board.

While it is not essential, I prefer to prime my boards both on the front and back. I am not always sure of the conditions the artwork will be subjected to.

PAINTING A BACKGROUND COLOUR

By painting the sides of your board before applying the resin, it gives your board a more professional finished look.

There are many ways to finish off your resin art sides, one of my favourites is to paint the sides first. Resin, when first poured, is quite runny and when it runs over the side, leaves a very thin layer of resin which is very transparent. Now you can wait until the resin starts to cure and goes sticky and using a heat gun, encourage it to move over the sides, or pick up resin drips from your table and re-apply it to the sides.

If you paint your sides in the base colour of your finished piece, there is no need to keep applying resin or to even fiddle with the sides. Just make sure you have an even coverage of resin, for a nice glossy finish.

This board was painted green before applying the resin, as you can see, there is good coverage of colour on the sides.

PREPARING THE EDGES

There are various ways in which you can prepare the edges of your board, it all comes down to what look you want to achieve.
Do you want the resin to run over the sides?
Do you want the resin on the top of the board only?

LEAVING THE EDGES

It is not necessary to tape the sides of your board, you can simply allow the resin to run over the edge as you pour it on the surface.

Note, freshly mixed resin, will run off the sides, leaving a very thin layer. If you want good colour coverage, you will need to reapply resin to the sides.

RESIN ON THE SURFACE ONLY

If you wish to have a clean finish on the sides with no resin, then tape the sides about 1-2mm from the top. This allows for a nice edge.

Leave the resin to cure for about 6 hours, then using a sharp knife, run the blade over top edge of the tape, then remove the tape. This will give a nice clean edge and won't 'rip' the resin.

Clean Crisp Sides can be achieved by taping the edge, remember to tape 1-2mm down from the top for a perfect finish.

preparing your board

CREATING A DAM

If you want good coverage of resin on the sides of your board, it is recommended that you create a dam on the surface. Using painter's tape or something similar, apply tape to the sides making sure your tape sits around 10-20mm above the resin surface.

Now when you pour your resin, it won't flow over the sides, instead, it remains on the surface of the board.

Leave the resin to cure for around half an hour (could be longer depending on your resin or room temperature). The resin should still be sticky.

It is recommended that you don't leave the tape on for too long. If your resin cures past the sticky stage, you will be left with a lip on the resin and it won't run over the sides. This will require you to sand the resin lip and you may have to apply a clear coat of resin on the surface.

Remove the tape and using a little heat around the edge, allow the resin to run over the side. Using a stick, help spread the resin over the surface of the edges, to ensure good coverage.

Note: it is essential that your board is level, otherwise you may find some areas don't have enough resin to cover the sides.

Make sure you have plenty of tape sticking up from the board and it is stuck down well.

PREPARING THE BACK

Just like the sides, you have different options for preparing the back prior to applying resin.
You can either apply tape to the back and once your resin is cured, add a little heat and remove the tape.

Or you can leave it as is and clean up the back with a heat gun and wood chisel. This is my preferred option because I like to get straight in with the resin pouring, it is while cleaning the back that I add the hanging hardware and add my signature.

Either way, it takes around the same length of time to tape the back, as it does to clean up afterward. So it is down to personal preference which option you prefer.

It is also a good idea to prime the back of your board as well as the front. This will prevent moisture from warping your board and give it a nice clean finish on the back.

Taping the backside of the board.

types of resin

There are many types of resin on the market, from adhesives to fiberglass resins. The main resins we are going to cover in this guide are related to what resins are best to use in your art and craft projects.

Which resin you need to use will depend on the project you want to create.

EPOXY RESIN

Epoxy resins are well know for their adhesive properties, making it a popular choice in many industries. It offers great heat resistance and is durable enough to use on wood, metal and fabric, making it a great choice for use as a protective covering for art.

Resin comes in two parts, the resin and the hardener. A chemical reaction occurs when the two parts are mixed together.

Not all epoxy resins are created equally and all will generally yellow over time. In order to extend the life of your resin art, it is recommended that you opt for a resin that contains good UV inhibitors. This reduces the yellowing of the resin.

COATING RESIN

Coating resins are mainly used for pouring on objects like artwork and table tops. They are generally much thicker than casting resins and are slow-moving, making them the ideal choice for your resin wall art or covering tables.

Coating resins are designed to be poured in thin layers and you will generally get up to 40 minutes working time. Although, this varies from brand to brand and your current room temperature, so always refer to the manufacturer's instructions.

Note: thicker layers will result in your resin overheating (exothermic reaction) and curing very fast. If you are just starting out with resin, it is recommended that you mix smaller batches of resin, especially until you are confident about working with resin.

Coating resins are generally much thicker than casting resins. While you can still use a coating resin to cast items, you have to pour in thin layers and wait 4-6 hours of curing between pours.

CASTING RESIN

Casting resins, by contrast, are much thinner and runnier than coating resins. They are also much slower in curing, which allows for larger amounts to be poured into moulds.

Due to the viscosity of this resin, it is also much easier to deal with bubbles when casting.

You still need to read the manufacturers instructions on how deep you can pour the casting resin into moulds, as this varies from brand to brand.

POLYESTER RESIN

Polyester resins don't cure well when poured in thin layers, so it is more suited as a casting resin.

Note: These resins are generally more pungent than epoxy resin. It is not recommended you use them in your home and certainly not without the right ventilation and protective safety gear. Plus, due to the complicated mixing procedure of this type of resin, it is not recommended for beginners. So I won't go into detail on this type of resin.

preparing resin

Now that you have prepared your board to take the resin, it is now time to prepare your area ready for the resin mixing.

BEFORE YOU START
Before you begin mixing your resin, collect together everything you will need for your project. Mixing cups, stirrers, colours (paint, powders, paste or inks), safety gear, old clothes and don't forget to cover your table and protect your floors.

Note: you have a limited time to work with resin, so it is best to get your area ready before you begin mixing.

LEVEL YOUR BOARD
To avoid unnecessary loss of resin, always make sure your board is level. If you don't have a spirit level, you can use your phone, if you don't already have an app, you can easily download one.

I make sure my table is completely level, this saves a lot of time when working with more than board at a time.

CALCULATING THE AMOUNT OF RESIN TO USE
You will find that most of the major resin manufacturers have a handy online resin calculator. Simply enter the size of your board and it will calculate the amount of resin you require. I personally use U Resin's online calculator.

MIXING RESIN
Before measuring out your Part A and Part B, double check the packaging to see what ratio your resin needs to be mixed. Most resins use the 1:1 ratio, which means, that you pour equal amounts of Part A and B.

If it is a 2:1 ratio, simply work out how much you will need in total for your board, then divide that amount by 3, this will give you 1 Part and then double it, to get 2 Parts.

For instance, if you require 300mls of resin for your board, calculate 1 Part by dividing 300 by 3 = 100mls, for 2 Parts, times 100 by 2 = 200mls. When measuring your resin, there are two ways in which you can do, by using a measuring jug or by weighing the resin. I prefer to use a measuring jog. Check with the manufacturer for their preferred method of measuring.

Tip the contents of both cups into a fresh cup. By doing this, you can re-use the cups and mix up a fresh batch if required.

Mix for the required time, I have found most resins require mixing for around 3 minutes. Always check the packaging for exact mixing times.

Make sure you scrape around the sides and the bottom of the cup when mixing, to ensure you don't miss any of the mixture.

If using a clear coat on your board, transfer the mixed resin to another clean cup and mix for a further 30 seconds, this will ensure you don't have any sticky residue on your finished artwork.

If you are mixing resin with any colours, you don't need to follow the last step, as you will already be giving the resin an extra stir.

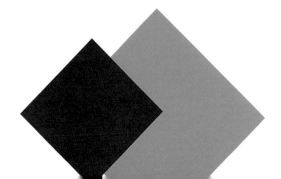

adding colour

There are many ways in which you can colour your resin before pouring on to your board. The general rule of thumb is to make sure you use less than 10% of the colour in your resin.

Less is definitely more, you don't need a lot of product to colour your resin if you are trying a new colour always start with a tiny bit. You can always add more if you need a stronger colour. Smaller amounts will give you a more transparent look.

TYPES OF COLOURS
There are a wide variety of colour products that can be used to colour your resin.

Note, I am referring to epoxy resin, polyester resins require specific colours that have been designed for polyester resin.

In this guide, I am going to give as much information as I can for each of the colourants you can use in resin.

POWDER PIGMENTS
Powder pigments are by far one of the best products to use in resin. If you buy from a quality supplier, you will find the pigments will mix really

easily with the resin and the colour saturation is second to none.

To mix, simply add a small amount of pigment into your cup, then pour a small amount of resin into the bottom, mix it into a paste, making sure you have no lumps of colour, before adding the amount of resin required for your project. Ensure you mix it well.

Note: make sure you wear a dust mask before opening and handling powdered pigments, especially the metallic pigments. You don't want to be breathing in the airborne particles.

PIGMENT PASTES
Pigment pastes are the same as powdered pigments, however, they have already been made into a paste to make it easier for you to mix with resin. Again, you only need a small amount of pigment to colour your resin.

ACRYLIC PAINT
You can mix acrylic paint in with resin, although, you need to be aware that too much paint can interfere with the curing process of the resin. I would recommend using as little paint as possible in your resin.

Tip: If you use higher quality paint, it contains more pigment, so you can use much less paint than the cheaper brands.

Note: Your working time will be greatly reduced when working with acrylic paint in your resin, so you need to work more quickly.

INK

Ink is great to use in resin if you are looking for a transparent look, for instance, if you are wanting to tint the resin to look like water.

Simply add one drop at a time and stir it until you get the colour you desire. Ink is very highly pigmented, so a little drop goes a long way.

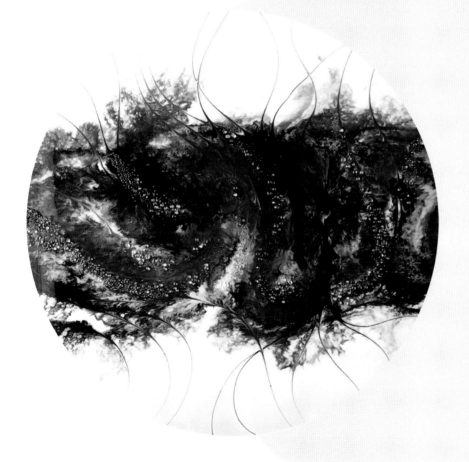

adding colour

MICA POWDERS

Just like the powder pigments, you can also use mica powders in your resin. Many people use eyeshadows in their resin with great results. This is to try out when you first get started with resin, as you can use cheap eyeshadows.

ALCOHOL INKS

Using alcohol inks in your resin makes for really interesting designs. Like regular inks, you only need a tiny drop in your resin to colour it.
You can also drop alcohol inks directly on to your resin and watch as it disperses and moves in the resin.

Note: Alcohol inks are not light-fast, meaning they fade very quickly, so if you are planning to sell your resin art, it is advisable to look into UV coatings to protect your art from fading.

OIL PAINTS

Oil paints can be used to colour resin. I would, however, recommend experimenting with small amounts of oil paint in your resin, simply because oil repels resin, so you may end up with unpredictable results.

SPRAY PAINTS

I like using metallic spray paints in my resin. Again, you only need a small amount of spray paint to colour your resin. A couple of squirts goes a very long way.

You can use spray paints in two ways, either mix it in with your resin and pour as normal, or add it to the surface with a stick. I like to use both methods, depending on what look I am wanting to achieve.

Remember to only use spray paints in well-ventilated areas, as I always wear a respirator when using resin, I don't worry too much about taking it outside, although, I do make sure I have good ventilation to help it disperse.

GLITTER

Glitter is a great product to add to your resin, it comes in many different colours and adds another dimension to your resin.

Unlike adding paints, powders or inks, you are not restricted to the 10% rule, because it doesn't interfere with the curing process.

I will go into more detail on adding other items, like glass, stones and texture into your resin later on in this guide.

PRODUCTS TO AVOID

You cannot use any paint products that contain a lot of water, water and resin don't mix. You will be left with a lumpy stringy mess.

Some high flow products, in particular, flow medium, that is used for acrylic pouring are not suitable for use in resin.

I believe glass paints also don't mix well with resin. I haven't yet tried glass paints, so I could be wrong.

If in doubt, always test a small amount in your resin, then leave it to cure to make sure it doesn't interfere with the curing process.

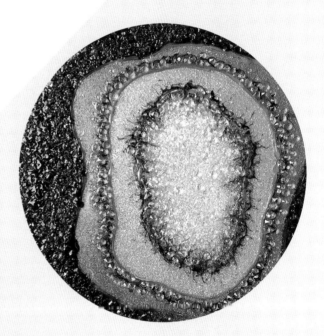

Silver and Turquoise Glitter.

choosing your colours

Choosing the right colour combination for your resin art can be quite a daunting task. If you look at what you were taught in school, Red, Yellow and Blue are the primary colours. If you mix them together, for instance, Red and Yellow = Orange, Yellow and Blue = Green and Red and Blue = Purple you will get your secondary colours. As an artist, you will soon discover that mixing these colours together in various combinations, will not get the results you desire. You will quite often end up with muddy colours and not the bright colours you were
hoping for.

CMYK
Having worked in the print industry for over 30 years. I very quickly realised that the primary colours used to achieve all the colours of the rainbow in print, actually comes from Cyan (C), Magenta (M) and Yellow (Y).

Note: Black is made up mixing CMY together. Black is referred to as the Key (K) colour in print.

Mixing Magenta with Yellow actually gives you Red and to get Purple, you need to mix Magenta and Cyan together etc.

If you were to mix Red and Blue together as they tell you to do in school, you are actually adding Yellow to the mix, this will actually give you a very dirty colour.

So as you can see putting into practice what you were taught in school can make things difficult.

Having said that, I am not saying that mixing the primary colours you learnt in school is wrong, you just need to be aware that you may not get the desired results, and that different shades of red and blue will yield different results.

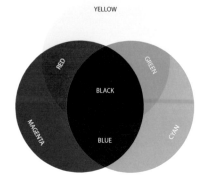

CYMK - Mixing Colours.

RGB

RGB or Red Green Blue and the colours that are used for televisions and computer screens. RGB has a larger colour range than CMYK, meaning not all of the colours you see on your screen can be printed. So for this reason, I am not going to refer to these colours for your resin art.

COLOUR MIXING

You don't need to own every single colour under the sun, while it is nice to have a full range of colours at your disposal, you can get by with a limited range of colours and mix them to get a wider range.

I would suggest having the primary colours of red, blue, yellow, plus magenta, cyan and of course white and black to make your tints and shades.

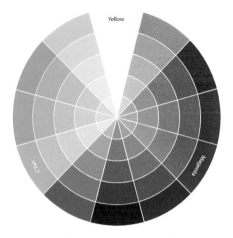

CYM Colour Wheel, from this all the colours you need can be made.

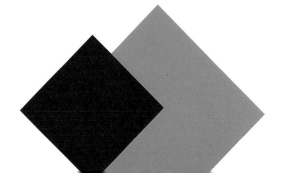

choosing your colours

CREATING YOUR COLOUR PALETTE

When starting out with resin or any art for that matter, choosing the right colours is essential before you begin.

It is not a good idea to mix your resin, then walk away and decide on what colours you are going to use. Once mixed, your resin begins to cure in the cup.

You have many options for colour combinations, here are a few ideas to get you started.

COMPLEMENTARY COLOURS

This is two colours on opposite sides of the colour wheel.

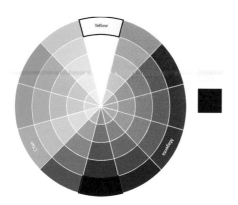

MONOCHROMATIC COLOURS

These colours come from the same family and are tints and shades of the same base colour.

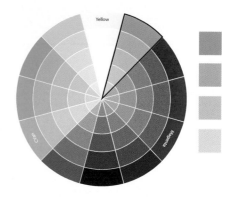

ANALOGOUS COLOURS

These colours sit next to each other on the colour wheel.

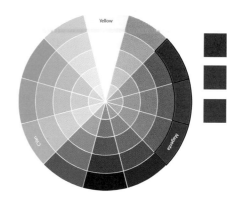

TRIADIC COLOURS

These colours are evenly spaced around the colour wheel and give a bold contrast to your colour palette.

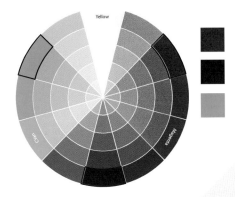

TETRADIC COLOURS

These are four colours that are evenly spaced around the colour wheel.

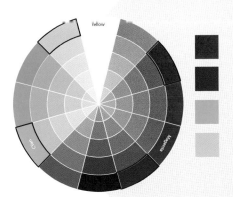

SHADES TONES AND TINTS

On top of all the different ways to choose your colours, you have many more options to contend with, shades tones and tints of colours by adding black, white or grey to the base colours.

Shades are achieved by adding black to the base colour. In contrast, tints are achieved by adding white to the base colour and tones are achieved by adding a combination of white and black, or grey.

ONLINE COLOUR PALETTE GENERATOR

If all of this feels a little daunting and you want a simple solution to choosing your colours. There are many online colour palette generators to help get you started.

Some generators allow you to upload a photograph and it will select the range of for you. This is handy if you like the colour scheme of a room or you want to replicate the colours in a landscape.

Other generators, allow you to pick the main colour and will put a palette together for you.

pouring resin

There are many techniques in which you can apply the resin to your board, from a straight pour to a dirty pour. Here I will share some of the more popular methods.

CLEAR COATING

Clear coating is when you apply a layer of resin over a painting, for instance, if you have created an acrylic pour and want to protect it and give it a glass-like, glossy finish, then a clear coating of resin is the way to go.

First, you need to make sure your painting is fully dry. It is recommended that you leave an acrylic pour to fully dry for at least a month.

It is also essential that there is no silicone or any other additive remaining on the surface. Silicone and oil repel resin, so it is important to take the time to make sure there is no residue left.

I go into more detail on how to clean silicone and other additives before applying resin, later on in this guide.

Elements added using clear resin.

STRAIGHT POUR

A straight pour is exactly what it says, you take the mixed resin, it can be tinted in any colour of your choice and apply it, straight from the cup, directly to your board.

After which, you can manipulate it in a number or different ways to achieve your desired results.

I go into more detail on how to work with resin later in this guide.

DIRTY POUR

A dirty pour is when you pour your mixed resin colours into one cup, it is usually done in a controlled manner, being careful not to mix and blend the colours.

It is at this stage that you can add a drop of alcohol between the layers or even some other additives to help enhance cell creation. Some people also give it a quick stir with a stick before pouring the entire contents on to the board.

Straight Pour.

Dirty Pour.

pouring resin

FLIP CUP

A flip cup is very similar to a dirty pour, you add the colours to a single cup, only instead of pouring the contents of the cup in a controlled manner around the board.

You quickly flip the cup and place it upside down onto the surface of the board and wait a few minutes for the resin to flow to the bottom, before removing the cup.

Depending on the size of your board, you may need to flip several cups.

You may also need to tilt your board to help the resin flow to the edges.

Note: Both the Dirty Pour and the Flip Cup process can give you very unpredictable results, how well they turn out is determined by a number of factors. For instance, the density of the colours used, the viscosity of the resin, what additives you applied and even how well the resin wants to move.

VARIATIONS

If you go on to YouTube, you will see many variations on the Dirty Pour and Flip Cup Pour.

For instance, after flipping your cup, you can cut slits in your plastic cup. This helps to add air to the cup and aid the release of resin from the cup, giving you a more controlled pour.

You will also find many other ways to pour, for instance using a strainer or even string.

Flip Cup Pour.

working on the sides

Many people struggle with getting resin on the sides of their board to look good. Freshly poured resin runs off the sides very quickly, leaving you with a very thin layer that doesn't look as vibrant as it does on the surface.

Earlier we talked about how to prepare your board for different looks on the sides of your board, now we are going to go into more detail on how to get that perfect look.

There are a number of ways you can achieve good resin coverage on the sides of your board and all of which relies on waiting for the resin to semi cure, just enough so that is has begun to get tacky, although, can still move.

CREATING A DAM

Creating a dam is probably the easiest way to wait for the resin to cure just enough.

By a dam, I mean, using tape to stop the resin from spilling over the sides of your board. Painter's tape and any equivalent tape works well for this.

When using this method, you need to ensure you have enough resin on the surface for when you remove the tape. If you don't have enough, you will end up with patchy areas.

I recommend, including the sides of the board in your calculations when working out how much resin you require.

Leave your resin to cure for about an hour. Maybe more depending on the temperature of the room, before removing the tape. If the resin is slow to move, apply a bit of heat to the edges to help with the flow.

A taped dam around the board.

working on the sides

PAINTED SIDES

Painting the sides of your board is another way to ensure good colour coverage of the edges of your board.

By painting it in a similar base colour to your finished piece, you take the pressure off yourself to achieve the perfect sides.

You will still get a nice glossy finish, providing you make sure the resin has covered it all. Make sure you run your hand around the edge to ensure good coverage.

USING THE RESIN RUNOFF

Another way to make sure you have good resin coverage on the sides is to use your resin runoff.

Wait for the resin to cure for about an hour, just like in the dam method, only this time, using a stick, pick up the sticky resin from your table and apply it to the surface next to the edges.

The reason I suggest applying it to the surface and not just to the edges is for two reasons. First, you are going to apply some heat to help it over the side and two, it self levels with the surface to give you a perfect blend to the top and sides of the board.

Note: If you leave the resin on the surface for as long as possible before guiding it over the edge, you will get a thicker flow occurring, this will reduce the amount of resin run off you will require, if any.

Sides were painted before the resin pour.

CRISP CLEAN SIDES

You, of course, don't have to have the resin running off the sides, you can opt for the clean crisp look and to achieve this, again involves taping the sides.

This time, instead of creating a dam, you will use the painter's tape to mask off the area that you don't want any resin on.

I would recommend applying the tape to the sides about 1-2mm from the top. This will ensure you get a nice rounded lip on the surface of your board. If you place the tape too high, when you remove it, you may end up with an uneven edge that you will have to fix.

Make sure your tape is fully bonded to the sides to prevent seepage under the tape. Use an old credit card to apply pressure to the tape to make sure it is stuck down properly.

It is best to leave the tape on until the piece has fully cured. Removing it too soon could result in drips from the semi-cured resin.

Before you remove the tape, run a very sharp blade over the top edge of the tape. You want to make sure you have cut through the resin where it has run over the edge of the tape.

Then apply a bit of heat to the tape, remove it from the edges. Done carefully, this will give you the perfect finish.

Crisp Clean Sides.

dealing with bubbles

When mixing your two parts of resin together, you are guaranteed to get bubbles. The quicker you mix your resin, the more bubbles you will get. The viscosity of your resin will also be a major factor on how bubbly your resin gets. The good news is, there are many ways to get rid of those pesky bubbles.

BLOW TORCH

Using a blow torch over the surface of your resin helps them come to the surface and pop. A quick glance over the surface is all you need.

Note: Don't hold the torch on the surface for too long, you will not only burn the resin, but you can burn the colours also.

HEAT GUN

A heat gun is a great alternative to the blow torch. It does take a little longer to pop the bubbles, however, you are less likely to burn your resin. Although, it is still possible, so don't hold it in one place for too long.

PRESSURE POT

If you are using a casting resin to make jewellery etc., then using a pressure pot can help eliminate bubbles.

As this guide is about pouring resin art on to various substrates, the pressure pot doesn't apply here.

Popping bubbles using a heat gun.

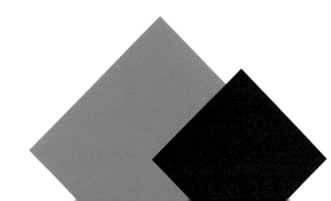

moving resin

There are many ways in which you can manipulate and move resin to create interesting shapes and effects.

FINGERS

The first method is to use your fingers, using your hands is a great way to spread the resin all over the whole board. It allows you to spread a thin layer, making it great for getting your base layer down.

I have also found that if you dabble your fingers across the surface, you can gently mix the resin without muddying it. This is ideal for creating ripples across the resin.

TILTING

If you don't want to mix the colours too much, but want to spread the resin all over the board, tilting the board is a good option. The great thing about resin, that even after you have tilted the board, the resin will self-level to give you an even layer of resin across the board.

Bear this in mind, as resin that has flowed to the edges will slowly run back across the board.

Resin shaped with the use of fingers.

moving resin

BLOWING

If you want to create a wispy effect with the resin, then blowing is a good option. For this method you will need a heat gun, airbrush or hairdryer in order to move it.

It is possible to move resin with a straw, however, it takes a great deal of strength to move it and you have to be mindful of not getting any saliva on the resin (water and resin does not mix).

BLOW TORCH

Applying heat across the resin can also aid the movement of resin, as it warms up, it begins to liquify further and this can help to move it.

Note: Be careful not to burn your resin when using a blow torch, also, make sure you wear a respirator as you heat the resin. It is likely to smoke and give off toxic fumes.

Blowing Resin with a Heat Gun.

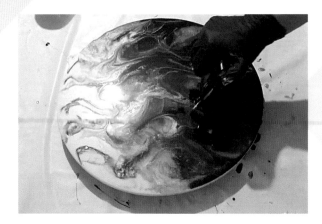

Blowing Resin with a Blow Torch.

SWIPE

Swiping is a great way to move resin if the conditions are right, this method can achieve lacing and cells in your resin.

In order to swipe your resin, it is best that you use something light with a flat surface. Things like a long blade spatula, baking paper or paper towels work very well.

DRAGGING

Using the flat side or edge of your stir stick can create great results. Lightly using the flat side of the stick acts in the same way as swiping, however, as it is placed on the resin on an angle, you don't get the same results as using the likes of baking paper.

The edge of a stick is great for creating details in your resin. If you leave your resin to cure for a little while, you can really get more control over the dragging. The resin doesn't blend too much and can leave you with defined lines.

Swiping the resin with a flat silicone spatula.

Dragging the white using a stick.

lacing and cells

There are many factors to take into consideration when trying to achieve lacing and cells. The viscosity of your resin, room temperature, how humid it is, the density of your pigments, pastes and paint and heat application, all play a major roll in creating lacing and cells.

Here is a quick breakdown of how I have achieved the elusive cells and lacing.

Note: What works one time, may not work the next. I have found it easier to achieve cells and lacing in the summer months when it is nice and warm and find near on impossible in winter. Heat obviously plays a major role.

SWIPE METHOD
The swipe method is by far the most popular method to achieve cells and lacing.

Simply place a range of colours together and using a paper towel, or baking paper and drag it across the surface. Add a touch of heat and watch the magic happen.

For best results, I will select a variety of different products for the project. For instance, I will not only use my go-to pigments and pastes, but I will also use inks and paints.

The reason for this is that each of the products has different densities and weights, so some will drop through the colours and others will rise to the top and give you cell formation.

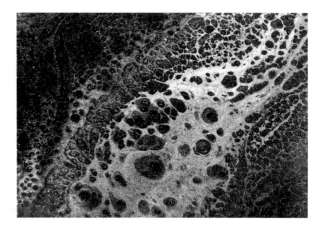

For this I used a mixture of metallic pigments, India ink and acrylic paint.

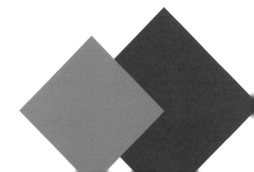

HEAT

As mentioned earlier, heat plays a major role in achieving lacing and cells. When applying heat, each of the components within the resin will warm up at different rates, the resin will liquify slightly, forcing it to move.

As you apply the heat, you will see the separate colours begin to react differently to each other and some colours will begin to sink, while others will rise to the surface and break the resin up and in turn give you cells and lacing.

The best tool for this method is the blow torch, although, you can achieve it with a heat gun, it takes a little longer.

Note: When applying heat, be careful not to burn your resin, especially when using the blow torch, it takes a bit of practice to apply just the right amount of heat.

ADDITIVES

Adding additives to the resin is another popular method to achieve cells and lacing. Some people swear by using silicone or oil. However, this method can leave dimples in your resin and will require additional clean up and more resin to fix.

I personally, like to use Mineral Turpentine to create lacing. The reason is, the turps evaporates and doesn't leave any imperfections in your resin.

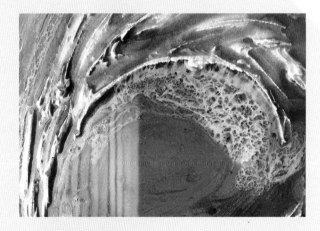

Here I added a couple of drops of turpentine to the white resin and applied it with a stick.

lacing and cells

LAYERING

Another way to create cells and lacing is by layering your resin.

You will put down your base layer and get it looking how you want it to look. Leave it to cure for a little while before adding the next clear layer.

Next, add your next colour (white is usually best for this method) and then move the resin by either using a heat gun or hairdryer.

Watch as lacing and cells begin to happen.

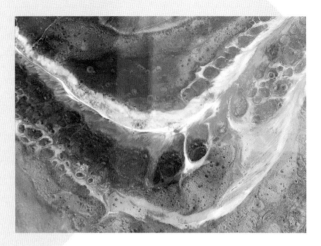

An example of using a clear resin layer then adding white to achieve a wispy look.

EXPERIMENTING

As I mentioned earlier, there are many factors in which to create cells and lacing. I highly recommend that you keep notes on how you achieve your cells.

For instance, what colours you used, the method you used, the time of year, what the temperature was like, was it humid? Was it raining? etc., etc. This will give you a better understanding of what works best for you.

adding texture

Adding texture to your resin can turn an ordinary pour into something different and special. I discovered texture very early on my resin journey.

I was struggling to achieve the fabulous r esults I was seeing everyone else achieve, so I started adding elements to the resin, to 'disguise' the mess.

Suddenly, everyone wanted to know what I was doing and I knew I was on to something.

GLASS AND GEMS

The quickest and easiest way to add texture to your resin art is to apply glass and gems to your art. These can be added at any time during the curing process and there are many ways in which they can be used.

You can simply drop them on to the curing resin, I find it is best to see follow the shapes in your resin, that way they don't look like an afterthought.

Or you can mix them in a tiny amount of resin before applying them to the board.

adding texture

GEODES

Geodes are a very popular way to incorporate glass and gems in your resin. Many people are familiar with Mrs Colorberry, it was her very first geodes that started the geode craze, now everyone who has ever done resin wants to create the perfect geode.

They are placed in a very controlled manner and the resin is added around the structure of the geode.

SAND

Sand is another good way to add texture to your resin. The depth of texture you can achieve is dependent on how much resin you mix with your sand.

For a course texture, add a tiny amount of resin and mix well with your sand, mix until your all the sand is coated. For a smoother finish, simply add a touch more resin until you have t he right consistency.

You can also use things like tile grout in resin.

LARGER ELEMENTS

Resin is essentially a glue, when cured, anything you add is well and truly stuck. With that in mind, you can add all kinds of fabulous things to your resin.

I have used Stones, Shells, Air Dry Clay and Potpourri, to name but a few, in my resin art. This takes your resin art to a whole new level, you are only limited by your own imagination.

Potpourri and texture paste in resin.

TEXTURE PASTE

In addition to adding elements into your resin, you can also create texture prior to pouring your resin. I have used this method for many of my projects.

There are many materials you can use to create texture. This includes modelling paste, ready mixed multipurpose filler (wall and wood filler are good alternatives). Tile grout and even your own homemade texture paste (made from PVA glue, talcum powder and paint), works very well.

The contrast between the rough texture and smooth glossy resin makes for a really interesting piece.

FABRIC

As resin is essentially a glue, it makes a fabulous fabric stiffener, making it a fabulous product to use with fabric.

By dipping fabric in resin and placing it on your board, you can shape in any way you want and it will give you a good backdrop to your art.

Tip: The more textured the fabric is, the better results you will get.

For this piece a mixture of elements were used to create the background.

working with layers

It is possible to create fantastic resin art with just one layer of resin. However, there comes a time when you want to create more depth and show multi-layers of resin.

As always, the optimum time to pour your second and subsequent layers of resin will depend on your particular resin, the temperature of the room etc., etc.

This guide is just that, a guide to what I have found to be the best time to work with resin, it is recommended that you experiment with your resin.

SECOND LAYER
The best time to pour your next layer of resin is when it has been left to cure for around 4-6 hours. The resin should be semi-cured and no longer sticky.

To test the resin, use the stick you used to mix the resin as your tester. You don't want to touch your curing art piece. If the resin on the stick is no longer sticky but will leave fingerprints (if touched without gloves), then it is ready to take another layer.

When the resin is in this semi-cured state, it doesn't require sanding, as the new layer of resin will stick to the surface without any issues.

If you have left your resin to semi-cure, it is recommended that you lightly sand the surface of the resin, remembering to sand the sides also.

Clean the surface of the sanded resin thoroughly, remove any dust particles and wipe down with rubbing alcohol.

This gives the resin 'tooth' to cling to and will avoid any areas where the resin is struggling to stick.

cleaning up residue

It is very important that you don't have any residue on the surface of either your painting or resin before pouring another layer of resin.

Residue comes from the use of silicone or oil in either your acrylic pour or in your resin. These additives repel resin and can leave you with unsightly dimples in the surface of your resin.

ACRYLIC POUR CLEANING

If you are wanting to clear coat an acrylic pour painting that has used silicone or oil in the process it is possible to remove without ruining your artwork.

DRYING TIME

First, you need to let your artwork dry for at least 4-6 weeks, the longer you leave it, the better. Although acrylic paint may be touch dry relatively quickly, it actually takes much longer to fully cure.

LIFTING

Next, you need to apply a generous amount of bicarbonate soda or baby powder to the surface of the painting. Use a soft brush to lightly move the powder across the surface of the painting. The powder will begin to clump up in areas of high residue.

Brush the powder off with a stiff brush and check the surface to see if there is still some residue remaining. If so, repeat the process.

CLEANING

Once you are satisfied that you have got as much of the residue off the surface, it is now time to gently clean it. Mild dish soap or baby shampoo works best. Apply a small amount of soap to a lint-free cloth and gently clean the surface of the painting.

Note: Before cleaning the surface, do a test clean on the side or back of your artwork. Check the cloth to make sure it is not lifting the paint.

Next, give the artwork a wipe over with rubbing alcohol, again check that it is not lifting the paint. Once you are happy that all the residue is removed, you are now ready to apply resin.

how to keep the dust off

Dust and bugs are a real problem for resin artists, there is nothing worse than thoroughly checking your piece before leaving the room and finding when you come back, that annoying bit of dust or worse still, a bug trapped in your resin.

Luckily there are a few things you can do to reduce the risk.

SPRAYING FLOOR WITH WATER
Before you begin, you can reduce the number of dust particles in the air by spraying a light mist of water in the air of your room. The weight of the water will help to remove floating particles. Spraying the floor also will help stop dust particles from becoming airborne.

Note: Do this about half an hour before using your resin, to ensure no water gets into your resin. As you know, water and resin don't mix.

MAKE A DUST BOX
After you have poured your resin and inspected it for dust or bugs, it is a good idea to cover your resin.

You can make these out of cardboard or if it is a large piece, you could make a frame to the size of your table and cover it in plastic.

DUST SHELVES OR CUPBOARDS
Another option if working with smaller pieces is to place your pieces into a cupboard and close the doors. Or make some dust free shelves, by covering the outside with plastic.

MINI GREENHOUSES OR TENTS
If your area is so dusty that none of the above would work, then why not invest in a 'resin booth', you can create it out of tents or mini greenhouses. If you keep the doors closed when not in use, this will reduce dust and bugs and will give you a great area to work in.

dealing with dust and bugs

So you have done everything you can to make sure there are no bugs or dust on your piece and you come back to find that they have managed to find your piece and settle right in the middle of your art.

What can you do to fix it? Thankfully, there are a couple of things you can do to fix it.

HIDE IT

My own personal favourite is to hide the problem. I am quite fortunate that I don't have a problem with foreign bodies in my resin. However, on the very odd occasion when I do have an issue, I will hide it.

As you may already know, I am a big fan of using texture in my resin, so this firstly hides any imperfections. Texture is great for disguising blemishes, you can mix some crushed glass or gems in resin and add them to the surface in a way that looks like it is part of the design.

DRILLING AND SANDING

If adding texture is not an option, you can opt to remove the offending item by sanding or drilling it out of the resin.

Once removed, this will require a fresh coat of resin to get back the shine. Don't worry if you had to drill the offending item out, once a new coat of resin is applied, you won't be able to see it.

Note: if using this method, don't forget to lightly sand your whole piece, to make sure you get good resin bonding to the lower layer.

Added texture hiding imperfections.

finishing the back

Once your resin has cured, it is now time to finish the piece off. Whether you decided to tape the back or not, cleaning the back will give your piece a nice professional look.

REMOVING THE TAPE
The tape is best removed within the first 24 hours, while the resin is still curing, it makes the tape much easier to remove.

There are a few things I like to do before removing the tape, the first step is to use a sharp knife and cut the resin where it meets the tape. This will allow for a nice clean line and will prevent the resin from ripping off the sides if it is still quite soft.

Now using your heat gun, gently heat the resin and the tape will come off without any issues.

REMOVING DRIPS
If like me you don't bother using tape on the backside of your board and prefer to remove the drips instead. The best method I have found is to again use your heat gun to heat the resin and then remove the drips with a wood chisel.

Some people prefer to use a scraper, however, I have found, a wood chisel has a good sharp edge, doesn't bend and flex and thus gives you a good clean cut on the edge of the resin and more control over the removal.

DREMEL TOOL
Many people swear by using a Dremel tool to remove the drips. I personally don't like this method because it is easy to damage the backside of your board.

SANDING
Sanding is another option for resin drip removal, although, this can be quite arduous and time-consuming.

Don't forget to wear a dust mask when sanding resin.

hanging artwork

While you are cleaning the back of your resin, it is now a good time to add the hardware to the back for hanging.

D-RINGS AND FIXINGS

Resin can be very heavy, especially the larger pieces. Some of my large rounds weigh around 7Kgs (15lbs approx.), so you need to make sure you use fixings that can withstand the weight.

Heavy duty D-rings are my preferred method, many galleries insist on D-rings as they work well with their hanging system. Make sure you use the right size to take the weight.

The D-rings need to be positioned about a third of the way down. The direction you have them pointing will depend on how they will be used.

For instance, some galleries, don't want you to have any hanging cord with them, as they hang using just the D-rings, so having the ring pointing upwards will work for this.

If adding hanging cord (again my preferred option) or wire, then face the rings into the centre of the board.

HANGING CORD OR WIRE

Again due to the weight of resin, it is recommended that you double up on the cord or wire.

Attach one end securely to one D-ring, thread it across the board, run it through the other ring and then bring it back to the first ring and again tie it securely.

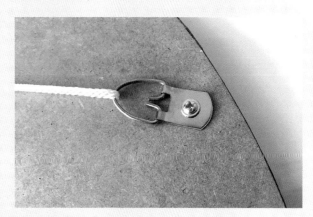

Heavy Duty D-Rings and Hanging Cord.

left over resin

Resin is quite an expensive hobby, so very often I am asked what you can do with leftover resin. Well, who wants to throw and waste their precious resin?

SILICONE MOULDS
The most popular method of using your leftover resin is to pour it into small moulds, for instance, small jewellery moulds work well with small amounts of leftover resin.

FREEFORM TRINKET DISHES
This is my preferred method of using up my left over resin. All you need is a bit of plastic or baking paper to pour your resin on to.

Leave it to cure until it is almost set. It is not sticky, although, you can still leave fingerprints. Drape it over a vase or upside glass, apply a little heat to help it bend, then leave it to cure overnight. Voila, you have a freeform trinket dish.

To make it even more interesting, you can add gems, stones or glass to the outer edges, or if you have enough left over resin, you can pour on another plastic sheet and then layer them on top of each other.

Ideas for creating freeform resin projects will available in my more advanced resin techniques book.

Multi-layer resin trinket dish, made from left over resin.

cleaning tools

Resin is a messy hobby and quite often can result in quite a bit of waste that ends up in a landfill. You can reduce the impact this has on the environment by re-using your tools wherever possible.

USING THE RIGHT TOOLS
Resin doesn't stick to silicone, so using silicone tools in your resin making, makes a lot of sense. They are easy to clean and can be used time and time again. Simply allow the resin to cure and then remove it from the silicone.

If you don't have access to silicone tools, you can still reuse plastic tools and cups. Again resin doesn't stick to plastic, so you can simply wait for the resin to cure then peel the resin off.

PLASTIC CUPS
There are a couple of ways you can clean your plastic cups and containers. You can leave your stick in the cup and when it is cured, pull the stick out and the resin will come away from the sides of the cup. This method doesn't always work, the stick may just come away, leaving the resin inside.

My preferred method is to let the excess resin run out on to plastic after it has removed the majority of the resin, turn the cup the right way up and allow the resin to cure. I don't try and remove the resin, I just leave it as it is and re-use with a similar colour next time.

MEASURING JUGS
To prevent a build-up of resin occurring within your measuring jug, it is best to clean it before it cures.

Let the resin run out on to the plastic and using a baby wipe, remove as much excess as possible. Then using rubbing alcohol or isopropyl, give the jug a good clean.

WOODEN STIRRERS
Wood sticks to resin and as such many people use the wood stir stirrers just the once, however, you don't have to. Once you have finished with your stirrer, place it on some plastic and let the resin cure. Cut off any excess resin around the stirrer and it is now good to use again. I have my stirrers for many months.

packaging and postage

When packing your resin for postage, there are few things you need to consider.

NO BUBBLE WRAP

Under no circumstances should bubble wrap be in contact with the surface of your resin. Bubble wrap reacts with the resin and can leave bubble indentations on your resin. This is made worse by heat and humidity.

After going to all the trouble of making sure your resin art is perfect, the last thing you need is your resin to arrive at its destination, damaged.

Bubble wrap is best used after you have used another form of protection on the surface of the resin.

GLASSINE

Glassine is a smooth glossy paper that is water and grease resistant. Glassine is an archival paper that is made from 100% sulphate and is frequently used by artists to interleave between their artworks for protection.

Wrap your resin in the glassine, before using any bubble wrap.

FOAM

Foam is a good alternative to glassine, because you don't have to worry about paint smudging on the surface. You can usually buy foam on a roll at your local hardware store.

DOUBLE WALLED CARTON

For the ultimate protection of your resin art, it is best that you use a double walled carton. This offers you the best protection, should the box get damaged.

Ensure your resin art is not moving freely in the box, as this could damage your work. Make sure any spaces are filled with either bubble wrap or newspaper, to ensure a snug fit and make sure you mark the box as fragile.

Note: I recommend that you wait a good 7-10 days before wrapping your resin art, resin continues to cure long after it is safe for you to handle. The longer you leave it, the better.

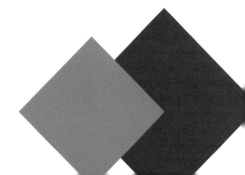

resin tips and tricks

We have covered many of these tips and tricks within this guide, however, you can use this area as a quick and easy guide to get started.

LEVEL SURFACE
Before embarking on your resin journey, make sure your table is lever before beginning.

PROTECT SURFACES
Make sure all surfaces are protected from the resin. This includes your floor and clothing.

BE PREPARED
Get everything ready before you start, this includes picking the colours you want to use. You only have a limited time to pour your resin.

MIX YOUR RESIN WELL
Make sure you mix your resin as directed by the instructions on the bottles. Poorly mixed resin may result in sticky spots of uncured resin.

REDUCE BUBBLES
Eliminate bubbles by allowing your resin to stand for a couple of minutes before pouring. Ensuring your resin is warm enough will also help and using a heat gun or blow torch will help pop any that come to the surface.

ALLOW RESIN TO CURE AT ROOM TEMPERATURE
Don't be tempted to try and have your resin cure at a faster rate, always leave it to cure at room temperature.

RESIN FINGERS
Use baby wipes to help with the removal of resin from your hands. Don't be tempted to use alcohol as this will cause the resin to be absorbed into your skin.

RESIN HAIR
If you get resin in your hair, use a touch of baby oil or tea tree oil to help remove it. Run it through the length of your hair and leave it for a couple of hours before washing it out. The resin should come away easily.

STORING RESIN
Avoid storing resin at very cold or hot temperatures, not only will it change the viscosity of your resin, it can also shorten its life.

resin tips and tricks

OBSERVE TEMPERATURES
Avoid using resin on very cold, wet or very humid days. This can affect the resin and cause curing issues.

MIXING RESIN
When starting out, only mix the resin in small batches, at least until you are familiar with your resin and feel confident that you can work within the pot life of your resin.

CHOOSING THE RIGHT RESIN
Not all resins are equal, it is essential that you choose the right resin for your project. Each resin has been developed for a specific purpose.

DON'T OVERESTIMATE YOUR ABILITIES
People on YouTube make pouring resin look easy, remember, they have had many, many hours of perfecting their craft. Always start small until you have become familiar with your brand of resin.

REMOVING HAIRS WHILE RESIN IS TACKY
If you spot a hair or imperfection, it is best to remove it while it is still tacky. Once removed, you can use heat to help liquify the resin to help itself level again.

WORKING WITH GLITTER
Although you wouldn't think it, glitter is heavy in resin and will sink to the bottom if poured straight away. Leave pouring your glitter resin until the very last minute or wait until the resin on the board begins to cure before adding your glitter.

WARMING YOUR RESIN WHEN COLD
Invest in a heat wrap, this will gently warm your bottles of resin. Many people use a bath of warm water to warm their bottles, however, you need to be careful not to get water in your resin.

resin composition

Now that you understand the basic fundamentals for creating your resin art, it is now time to create your masterpiece.

START WITH THE BASICS
When starting out, I recommend starting with a very basic colour palette. A maximum of three colours is all you need.

I recommend marking out your board on how you want your basic design to look. It doesn't matter if your design changes halfway through, mine often does at it develops. However, you have an idea and you can develop it from there.

START SMALL
Don't try to attempt a complicated river table on your first attempt at using resin, not only are you likely to be disappointed with the results, you will have wasted a lot of resin in the process. If you start small, you will get a feel for the resin and what it can do and you won't waste lots of your precious resin when you make a mistake.

We all make mistakes.

OVERWORKING YOUR RESIN
One of the biggest issues many resin artists have is with overworking your piece. We have all been there, your resin is coming together nicely, you like what you are seeing and then you keep going and before you know it, you end up with a muddy mess.

Sometimes it is hard knowing when to stop. Keep your design simple.

A very simple layout using just three resin colours.

resin composition

FIXING A MUDDY MESS

If you have been left with a muddy mess, there are a couple of things you can do. The easiest thing to do is to add elements to your resin, like glass or stones to give your piece a focal point.

This doesn't involve using more resin and is usually enough to give your piece the wow factor.

ENHANCING THE ORIGINAL LAYER

Another option is to add another layer to your resin. Leave the layer to cure for about 4 hours, before pouring again. I would recommend pouring a clear layer first, then adding a contrasting colour. The clear layer will help define your background and the new c ontrasting layer.

RE-POURING YOUR RESIN

If you really don't like your original resin pour and you feel it can't be salvaged by either adding elements or pouring a contrasting layer. All is not lost, you can simply start again and pour over the top.

In this case, I would recommend, painting a base colour over your original pour to give you a new fresh blank canvas. That way you can draw your new design on the top and you are not put off by the original pour.

Example of a muddied mess that was salvaged by adding texture.

about the author

My mission is to brighten the world, one art piece at a time.

I was around 4 or 5 when I first discovered I could draw and learnt my first life lesson. I was in school watching a film about wildlife in Africa, afterwards, our teacher told us to draw our favourite animal from the film.

I chose to draw a big strong elephant, it was quite a simplistic drawing, however, my fellow classmates were all praising my efforts, so much so, I was asked if I would draw their elephant for them. Being the helpful soul I am, I obliged and drew about 4 or 5 more elephants.

The next day, my teacher, asked who had drawn the elephants and feeling quite proud of myself, I threw my hand up in the air and said it was me. Next thing I found myself standing on the chair with my hands on my head as a punishment.

Fighting back the tears, trying to work out what I had done wrong. My teacher explained that it was okay to **SHOW** my fellow classmates how to draw, but if I do it for them, how will they learn to do it for themselves. - That lesson has stuck with me for the past 40+ years.

Fast forward to today, the majority of my working life has been spent as a Graphic Designer, creating art in the digital world.

In 2015, I rediscovered my passion for art and began experimenting with new and exciting art forms, from mixed media and scratchboards to polymer clay and art resin. I am constantly striving to get out of my comfort zone, work on different mediums and see where they take me.

My first ever lesson has stayed with me all these years and I still enjoy showing other artists how to create what I am creating.

I hope you enjoyed this beginners guide and it helps you on you on your resin journey.

notes

Printed by Amazon Italia Logistica S.r.l.
Torrazza Piemonte (TO), Italy

10642393R00031